W9-BAX-254

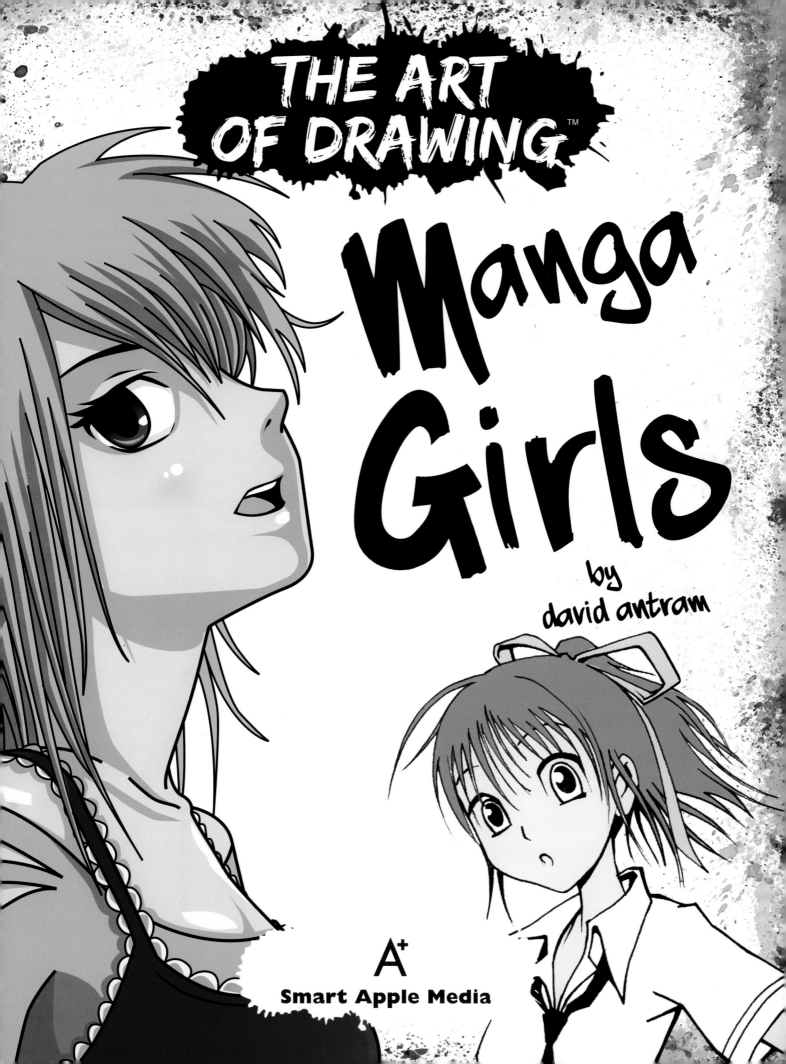

Published by Smart Apple Media,
an imprint of Black Rabbit Books
P.O. Box 3263, Mankato, Minnesota 56002
www.blackrabbitbooks.com

Published by arrangement with
The Salariya Book Company Ltd

Cataloging-in-Publication Data is available
from the Library of Congress

Printed in the United States
At Corporate Graphics,
North Mankato, Minnesota

9 8 7 6 5 4 3 2 1

ISBN: 978-1-62588-350-6

contents

making a start

The key to drawing well is learning to look carefully. Study your subject until you know it really well. Keep a sketchbook with you and draw whenever you get the chance. Even doodling is good—it helps to make your drawing more confident. You'll soon develop your own style of drawing, but this book will help you to find your way.

Practice drawing stick figures for basic poses...

...then dress them and add details.

quick sketches

Try sketching details from books or magazines.

perspective

Perspective is a way of drawing objects so that they look as though they have three dimensions. Note how the part that is closest to you looks larger, and the part furthest away from you looks smaller. That's just how things look in real life.

The vanishing point (V.P.) is the place in a perspective drawing where parallel lines appear to meet. The position of the vanishing point depends on the viewer's eye level.

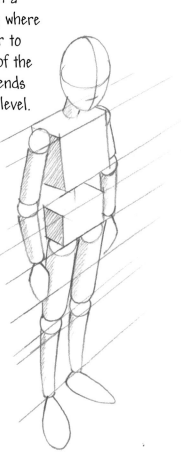

V.P.

two-point perspective drawing

Two-point perspective uses two vanishing points: one for lines running along the length of the subject, and one on the opposite side for lines running across the width of the subject.

In this drawing the vanishing points are very low down. This gives the impression that you are looking up at the figure— very dramatic!

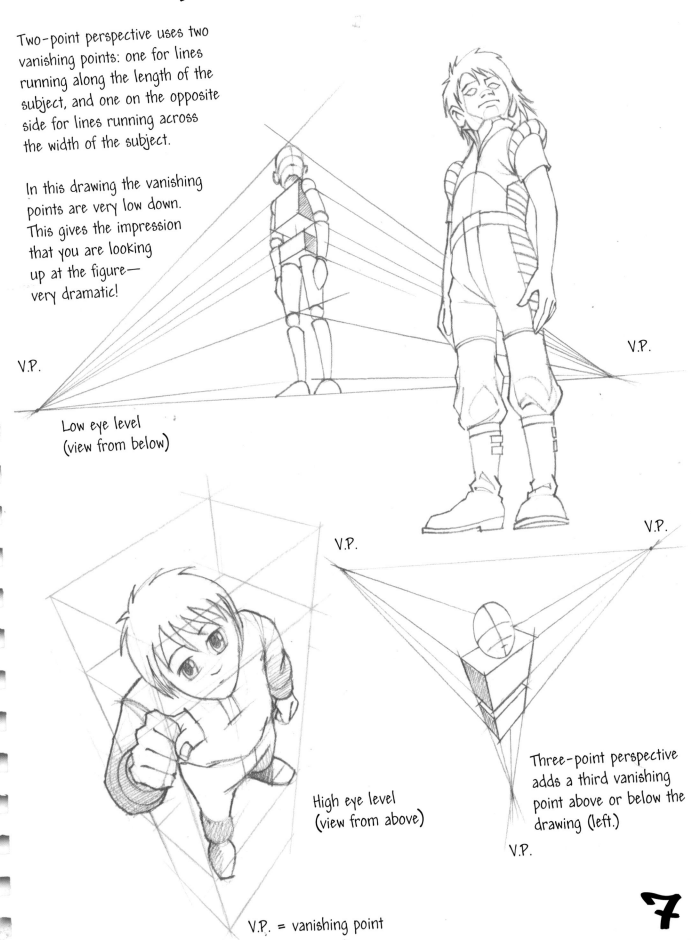

V.P.

V.P.

Low eye level
(view from below)

V.P.

V.P.

V.P.

High eye level
(view from above)

Three-point perspective adds a third vanishing point above or below the drawing (left.)

V.P.

V.P. = vanishing point

7

materials

Remember, the best equipment and materials will not necessarily make the best drawing—only practice will.

pencils

Try out different grades of pencils. Hard pencils make fine gray lines and soft pencils make softer, darker marks.

erasers

are useful for cleaning up drawings and removing construction lines.

paper

Bristol paper is good for crayons, pastels, and felt-tip pens. Watercolor paper is thicker; it is the best choice for water-based paints or inks.

Use this sandpaper block if you want to shape your pencil to a really sharp point.

inks

Use colored inks straight from the bottle or dilute them with water.

felt-tip pens

Felt-tips usually come in sets of mixed colors. The ones that make very thin lines are called fineliners.

Ink

Mixing palette

Fineliners

Dip-in pen nibs

Brushes

Correction fluid

Gouache

pens

Technical drawing pens have cartridges which can be refilled or replaced. Old-fashioned dip-in pens are much cheaper and come in many different styles and sizes.

Watercolors

paints

Ordinary watercolors are translucent (see-through); gouache is not. Try other kinds of paints, too.

Technical drawing pens

9

styles

Try different types of drawing papers and materials. Experiment with pens, from felt-tips to ballpoints. They will make interesting marks. What happens if you draw with pen and ink on wet paper?

Silhouette is a style of drawing which mainly relies on solid dark shapes.

Felt-tips come in a range of line widths. The wider pens are good for filling in large areas of flat tone.

10

Pencil drawings can include a vast amount of detail and tone. Try different grades of pencil to get a range of light and shade effects in your drawings.

Lines drawn in **ink** cannot be erased, so unless you are very confident you may want to sketch your drawing in pencil first.

It can be tricky adding light and shade to a drawing with a pen. Use a solid layer of ink for the very darkest areas and cross-hatching (straight lines criss-crossing each other) for ordinary dark tones. Use hatching (straight lines running parallel to each other) for midtones.

Hatching   Cross-hatching

11

body proportions

H eads in manga are drawn slightly bigger than in real life. Legs and hips make up more than half the overall height of the figure.

Center of balance

Drawing a stick figure is the simplest way to make decisions about a pose. It helps you see how different positions can change the center of balance.

Standing straight

Weight on right leg

Weight on left leg

Proportions of a female character

The eye level is about midway down the head.

Shoulders

Hips

Knees

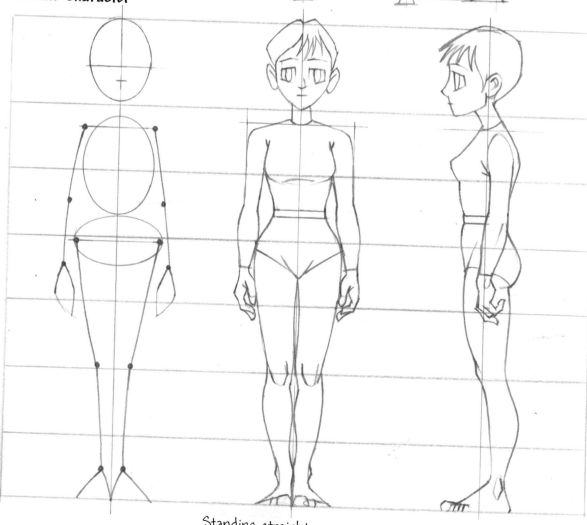

12 Feet

Standing straight

inking

Here's one way of inking over your final pencil drawing.

Refillable inking pens come in various tip sizes. The tip is what determines the width of the line that is drawn. Sizes include: 0.1, 0.5, 1.0, 2.0 mm.

Different tones of ink can be used to add depth to the drawing.
Mix ink with water to achieve the tones you need.

Correction fluid usually comes in small bottles or in pen format. This can be useful for cleaning up ink lines.

heads

Manga heads have a distinctive style and shape. Drawing different facial expressions is very important—it shows instantly what your character is thinking or feeling.

1. Start by drawing a square. Fit the head, chin, and neck inside it to keep the correct proportions.

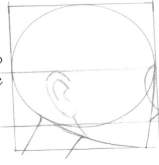

2. Draw two construction lines to position the top of the ear and the base of the nose.

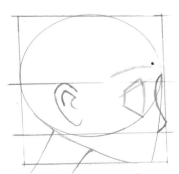

3. Add an oversized manga-style eye.

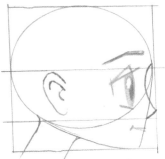

4. Add a pupil to the eye and draw the mouth.

5. Draw some manga-style hair.

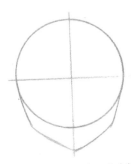

1. Draw a circle. Add construction lines through its center point.

2. Using the construction lines, position the eyes, ears, and mouth.

3. Add details.

4. Draw the hair.

14

Practice drawing heads from different angles and with different facial expressions.

Dreamy

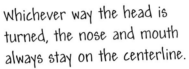
Centerline

Whichever way the head is turned, the nose and mouth always stay on the centerline.

Sad

Surprised

Shocked

Curious

Fascinated

Male heads, by contrast, have thicker necks and a squared-off, chiseled jawline. They also have slightly smaller eyes than females and wider mouths.

creases and folds

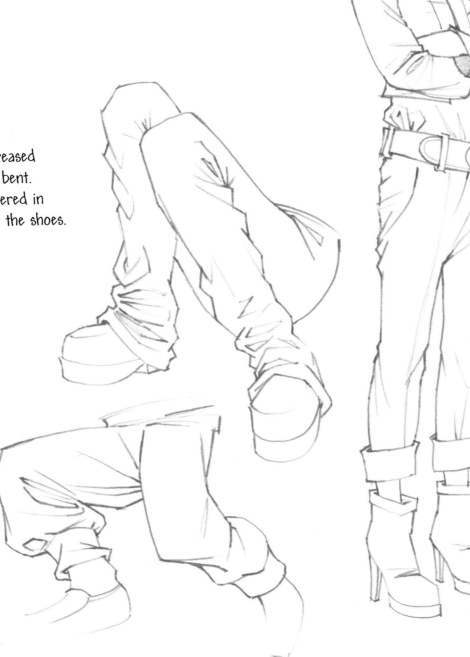

Clothes fall into natural creases and folds when worn. Look at real people to see how fabric drapes and how it falls into creases. This will help you to dress your characters more realistically.

These trousers have creased because the knees are bent. Excess fabric has gathered in folds and creases over the shoes.

Drawing from life can help you understand where and why creases and folds occur.

16

The way fabric is drawn can instantly give a sense of movement and action to a pose.

Study fashion magazines to get ideas for clothes and to see how different materials may look when worn.

neko girl

Neko is Japanese for "cat." This character has catlike ears and a tail on an otherwise human body.

1. Draw ovals for the head, body, and hips. Add center lines to divide the head vertically and horizontally. These will help you to place the ears and the nose.

2. Add lines for the spine and the angle of the hips and shoulders.

3. Draw stick arms and legs, with dots where the joints are. Add outline shapes for hands and feet.

4. Sketch the teddy bear in the same way.

5. Using the construction lines as a guide, start to build up the main shapes and features.

Cat ears

These little circles are to remind you where the elbows and knees go.

Cat tail

18

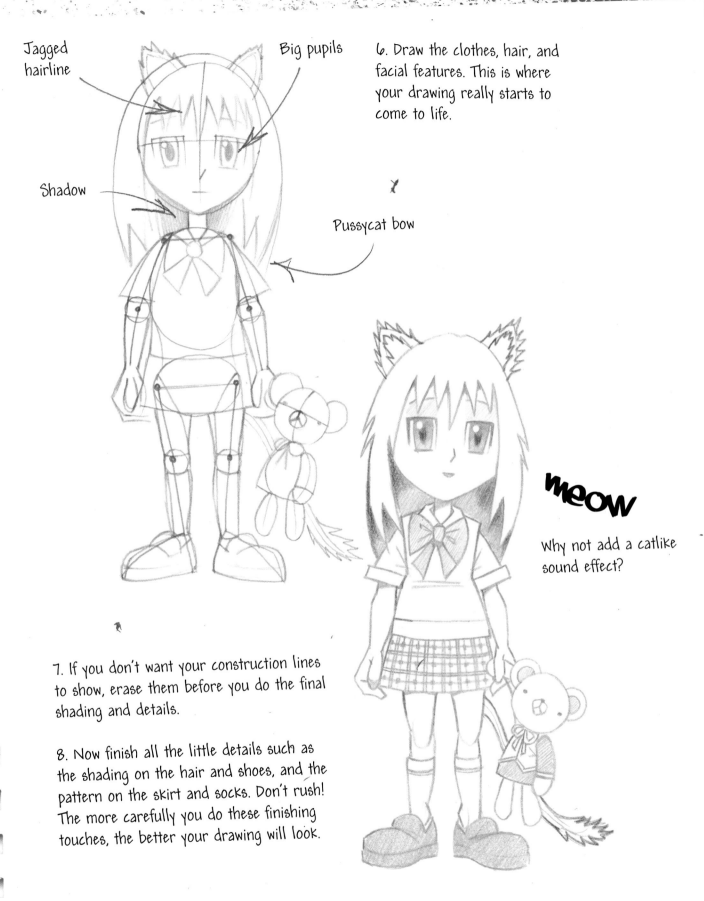

Jagged hairline

Big pupils

Shadow

Pussycat bow

6. Draw the clothes, hair, and facial features. This is where your drawing really starts to come to life.

meow

Why not add a catlike sound effect?

7. If you don't want your construction lines to show, erase them before you do the final shading and details.

8. Now finish all the little details such as the shading on the hair and shoes, and the pattern on the skirt and socks. Don't rush! The more carefully you do these finishing touches, the better your drawing will look.

high-class girl

This character may behave like a spoiled brat. She has the pride and social standing of a girl from a privileged background. She can be extremely bad-tempered and sometimes feels lonely.

1. Draw a circle for the head and ovals for the body and hips.

2. Add lines for the spine and the angle of the hips and shoulders.

3. Draw stick arms and legs with dots for the joints

4. Use your guidelines to sketch in the neck and facial features.

5. Using the construction lines as a guide, start drawing in the main shapes of the body.

Small circles indicate the positions of elbows and knees.

Lengthen the legs to give a more dramatic perspective— just like fashion designers do!

20

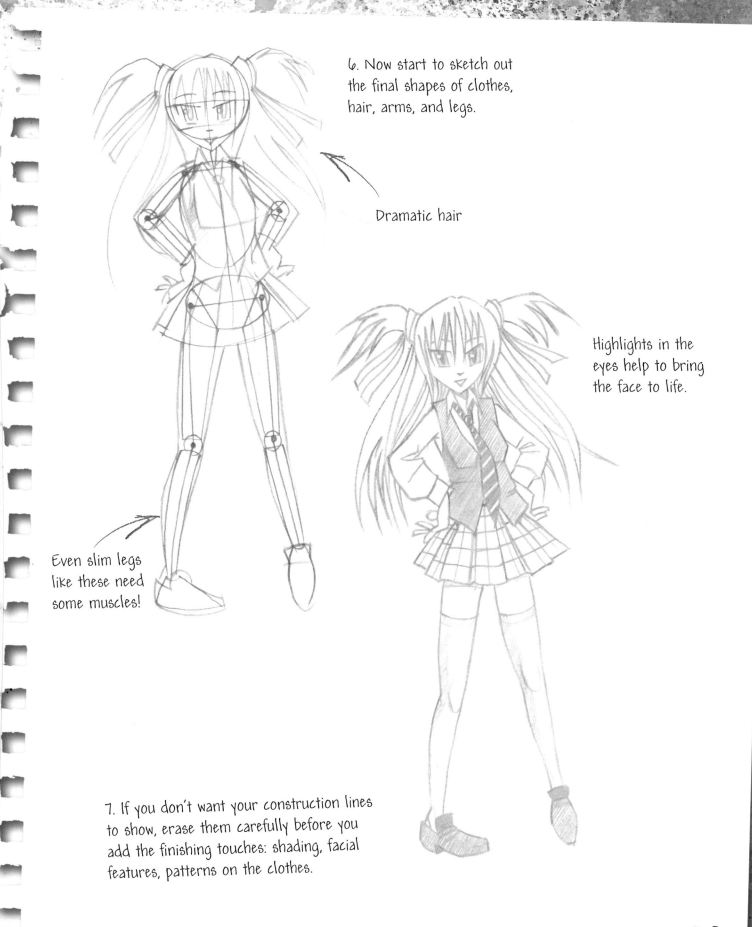

6. Now start to sketch out the final shapes of clothes, hair, arms, and legs.

Dramatic hair

Highlights in the eyes help to bring the face to life.

Even slim legs like these need some muscles!

7. If you don't want your construction lines to show, erase them carefully before you add the finishing touches: shading, facial features, patterns on the clothes.

shy girl

The shy girl enjoys reading (especially horror!) and dreams of becoming a writer.

1. Draw circles for the head and hips and an oval for the body,

3. Draw stick arms and legs with dots for the joints.

4. Using your construction lines, add the neck and sketch in the facial features.

2. Add lines for the spine and the angle of the hips and shoulders.

Remember to draw both legs, even though one is almost hidden from view.

5. Flesh out the arms and legs, using circles to indicate elbows and knees.

7. Erase your construction lines if you don't want them to show.

8. Take plenty of time to finish the details of the face and hair, the laced bodice and the fringed skirt.

Try to make the skirt fringe neat and regular.

6. Draw the shapes of the billowing skirt, the boots, bodice, and hair.

Heavy bangs

Flowing hair

Long, elegant fingers help to give her character.

Note how the long gloves crease at the elbows.

Shading shows which leg is in front and which one is behind.

eyes

Draw the eye shape and then add the pupil.

Either leave the highlights white, or paint them white using gouache or correcting fluid.

Highlight

magical girl

This girl may possess superhuman abilities and often has a secret identity. She fights evil and protects the Earth.

1. Draw different-sized ovals for the head, body, and hips.

2. Add a line for the spine and others to show the angle of the hips and shoulders.

3. Draw stick arms and legs with dots for the joints and outline shapes for the hands and feet.

Lines and small circles show the positions of the fingers.

4. Using your construction lines as a guide, draw the main shapes of the body and the position of the facial features.

In this pose, the graceful positions of the hands and feet are particularly important. Get the basic shapes right before you move on to the details.

24

The position of the thumb is important.

5. This figure wears a traditional Japanese costume. Draw the sleeves and skirt of the kimono, using angular lines to create folds in the fabric. Draw the face and the fluttering hair.

Note the wide draped sleeves, the collar, and the decorative sash and bow.

Although the legs are hidden, the kimono is shaped by them.

Try to get nice flowing lines in the hair.

6. Erase the construction lines if you want to, then draw the draped folds and tucks in the costume. Finish off all remaining costume details and add shading.

You could try finishing this drawing in ink.

The girl's legs bend slightly at the hips and knees. The shadow on the skirt is an effective way to show this.

cheery girl

The cheery girl is easygoing and lives alone. She enjoys her privacy, yet she makes friends with absolutely anyone.

1. This time you have the challenge of drawing two figures together! Draw the different-sized ovals and the other construction lines in the usual way. Notice how the backs of the two girls touch.

Notice that the overall shape of the two figures makes a triangle or pyramid.

Note how all the feet are at different angles.

2. Draw in tube-shaped arms and legs with circles for the knees and elbows.

3. Position the facial features.

Don't forget to use your construction lines as a guide when drawing the basic shapes of the body.

26

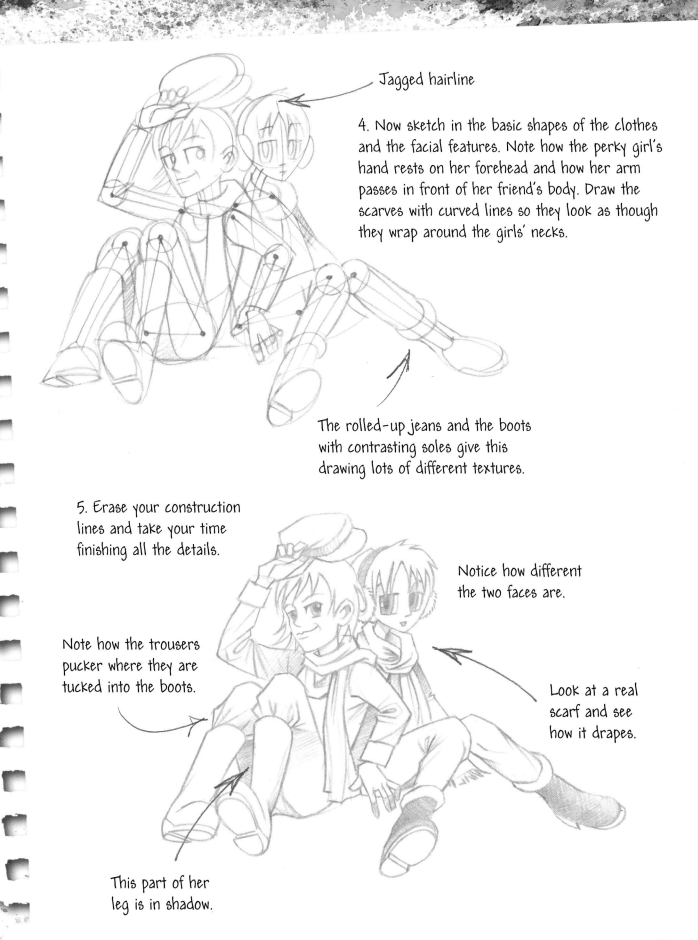

Jagged hairline

4. Now sketch in the basic shapes of the clothes and the facial features. Note how the perky girl's hand rests on her forehead and how her arm passes in front of her friend's body. Draw the scarves with curved lines so they look as though they wrap around the girls' necks.

The rolled-up jeans and the boots with contrasting soles give this drawing lots of different textures.

5. Erase your construction lines and take your time finishing all the details.

Notice how different the two faces are.

Note how the trousers pucker where they are tucked into the boots.

Look at a real scarf and see how it drapes.

This part of her leg is in shadow.

stylish girl

With her relaxed and dreamy expression, this girl is as elegant as a fashion model.

I. Draw the various ovals and construction lines as you have done before. Note how the right elbow sticks out in an exaggerated way to emphasize the hand-on-hip pose.

Long, slender neck

2. Add the limbs and the facial features, paying attention to your construction lines. To give the effect of a fashion drawing, the hips are slimmer and the neck much longer than they would be on an actual person.

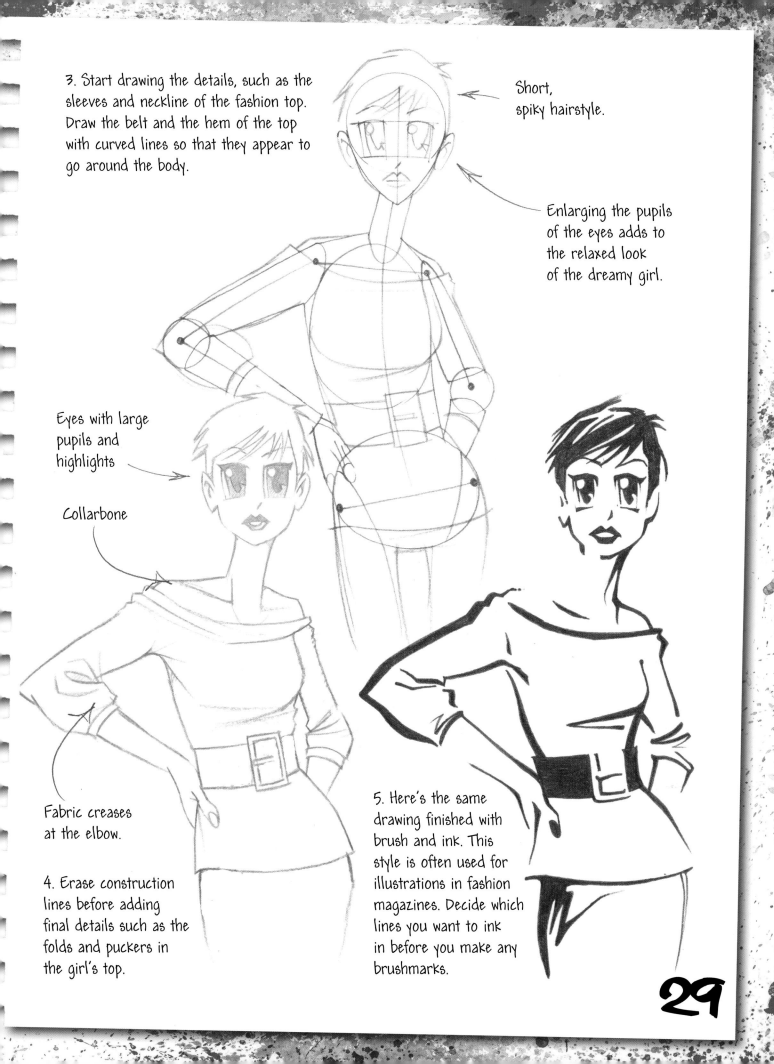

3. Start drawing the details, such as the sleeves and neckline of the fashion top. Draw the belt and the hem of the top with curved lines so that they appear to go around the body.

Short, spiky hairstyle.

Enlarging the pupils of the eyes adds to the relaxed look of the dreamy girl.

Eyes with large pupils and highlights

Collarbone

Fabric creases at the elbow.

4. Erase construction lines before adding final details such as the folds and puckers in the girl's top.

5. Here's the same drawing finished with brush and ink. This style is often used for illustrations in fashion magazines. Decide which lines you want to ink in before you make any brushmarks.

29

geeky girl

This girl's a bit of a tomboy, and is given to making unembarrassed naughty comments. She can be a worrying presence for those around her.

1. Draw the basic ovals and construction lines as usual. Try to get as much contrast as possible between the poses of the shy girl and her more confident friend.

The elegant shapes of the fingers are especially important.

2. Sketch the arms and legs and the main facial features. Note how the two heads face in different directions: one is in profile (side view) and the other is turned partly towards the viewer. Contrasts like this make a picture much more interesting—and lifelike.

3. Draw the details of the clothes and shoes. Try to get lively, swinging shapes in the hair.

We are going to finish this drawing in silhouette, so concentrate on details that will help to make the outline more interesting, such as the fringe, ponytail, fingers, and shoelaces.

Details such as the belt, the sandal straps, and the tops of the socks can be left white.

4. Silhouette is a very effective style. It looks easy, but to make a silhouette work all the small details of the drawing need to be thought out carefully before applying the ink.

31

glossary

Composition The positioning of the various parts of a picture on the drawing paper.

Construction lines Guidelines used in the early stages of a drawing which are usually erased later.

Cross-hatching A series of criss-crossing lines used to add shade to a drawing.

Hatching A series of parallel lines used to add shade to a drawing.

Manga A Japanese word for "comic" or "cartoon"; also the style of drawing that is used in Japanese comics.

Neko The Japanese word for "cat"; also a manga character that is part-human, part-cat.

Silhouette A drawing that shows only a dark shape, like a shadow, sometimes with a few details left white.

Three-dimensional Having an effect of depth, so as to look like a real character rather than a flat picture.

Tone The contrast between light and shade that helps to add depth to a picture.

Vanishing point The place in a perspective drawing where parallel lines appear to meet.

index